Heirloom Lace

A PATTERN COLLECTION

by Kerin Dimeler-Laurence

Printed in the United States of America

Second Printing, 2014

ISBN 978-1-62767-048-7

Versa Press, Inc
800-447-7829

www.versapress.com

CONTENTS

ORENBURG STOLE

by Kerin Dimeler-Laurence

FINISHED MEASUREMENTS
16" wide, 74" long

YARN
Knit Picks Shadow (100% Merino Wool; 110 yards/50g): Oregon Coast Heather 23656, 4 hanks.

NEEDLES
US 6 (4 mm) 40" or longer circular needles plus 2 double pointed needles or short circular for working Border, or size to obtain gauge

NOTIONS
Tapestry Needle
Stitch markers

GAUGE
19 sts and 40 rows = 4" in lace pattern, blocked

Orenburg Stole

Notes:

Worked lengthwise, this Orenburg-inspired stole has a bold geometric pattern.

DIRECTIONS

Loosely CO 340 sts using circular needles. Work in Garter st (knit every row) for 10 rows. On the next row, begin working lace: K5, PM, begin working from the Orenburg Quadrant 1 Chart on RS row 1, then at stitch 56 continue to the Quadrant 2 Chart. Repeat these 110 sts three times, placing markers between each repeat if desired, then PM and K5.

Work through all 74 rows of the Orenburg Quadrant 1 and 2 Charts, then rows 75 through 146 of the Quadrant 3 and 4 Charts, keeping the first and last 5 sts of each row in Garter st as established.

Work 10 rows in Garter st. BO all sts loosely kwise.

Border

Start the Border in the center of one side; this will make the join less obvious.

Loosely CO 6 sts using DPN's. Begin working from the Border chart on RS row 1. On each RS row, work the last P2tog st by slipping the last Border st Pwise, picking up a st Pwise from the edge of the Stole, and then purling those two sts together, joining the edging with the body. You will PU and purl in every two out of three sts along the length of the Stole body, and three out of every four Garter ridges on the shorter sides.

Corners

When you are two stitches or two rows (one garter ridge) from a corner, work four rows of the chart into each stitch or row by purling the edge stitches of two consecutive RS rows into the same stitch or row of the Stole. Work four rows into the corner in the same manner, and then repeat with the next two rows or stitches of the adjacent side; 20 rows of the Border will be worked into 5 picked up stitches at each corner.

When you have worked all the way around the Stole, you should be on Row 7 of the chart. Begin checking for this halfway through the last side. If needed occasionally PU in every stitch/row of the Stole, rather than in every stitch. BO the first three sts as shown, then break yarn leaving a generous tail. With this yarn tail, graft the remaining 6 live sts to the cast on row at the beginning of the edging.

Finishing

Weave in ends, wash and block.

Legend:

yo
⊙ RS: Yarn Over
WS: Yarn Over

k2tog
◻ RS: Knit two stitches together as one stitch
WS: Purl 2 stitches together

knit
◻ RS: knit stitch
WS: purl stitch

ssk
◻ RS: Slip one stitch as if to knit, Slip another stitch as if to knit. Insert left-hand needle into front of these 2 stitches and knit them together
WS: Purl two stitches together in back loops, inserting needle from the left, behind and into the backs of the 2nd & 1st stitches in that order

purl
⊡ RS: purl stitch
WS: knit stitch

No Stitch
◼ RS: Placeholder - No stitch made.
WS: none defined

p2tog
◻ RS: Purl 2 stitches together
WS: Knit 2 stitches together

⌐ Bind Off

How to read the charts

There are four quadrants making up the large repeat of this pattern. The first 74 rows are in quadrants 1 and 2, and rows 75 to the end are in quadrants 3 and 4.

All charts are read bottom to top; read RS rows from right to left and WS rows from left to right.

Quadrant 4 (Rows 75-145, sts 56-110 of repeat)	Quadrant 3 (Rows 75-145, sts 1-55 of repeat)
Quadrant 2 (Rows 1-74, sts 56-110 of repeat)	Quadrant 1 (Rows 1-74, sts 1-55 of repeat)

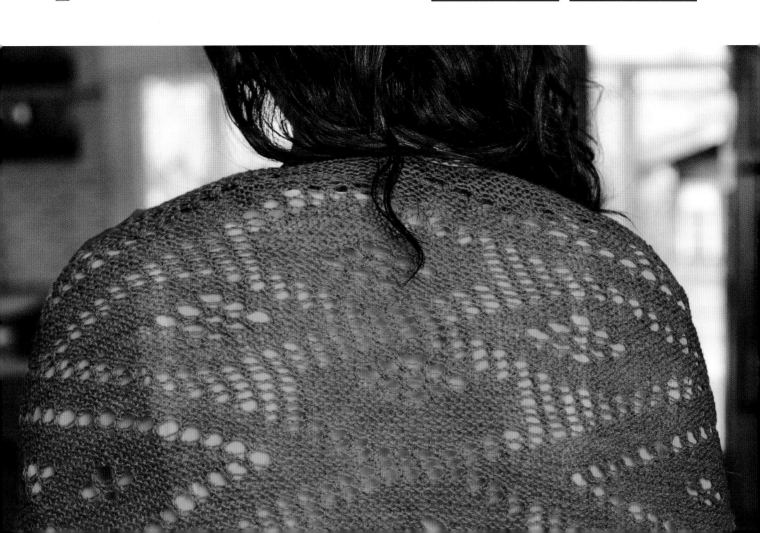

Orenburg Chart, Quadrant 2

Orenburg Chart, Quadrant 1

Border

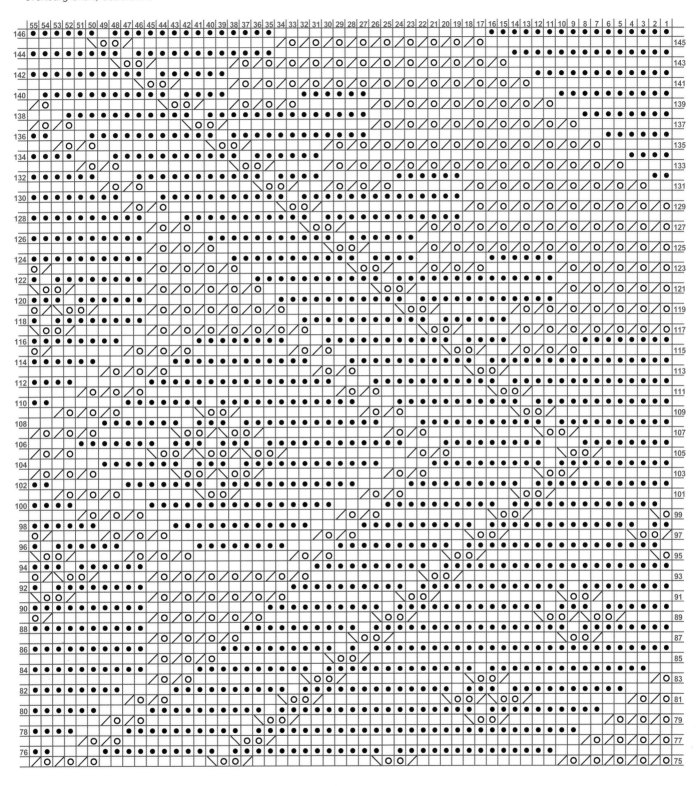

ESTONIAN SQUARE SHAWL

by Kerin Dimeler-Laurence

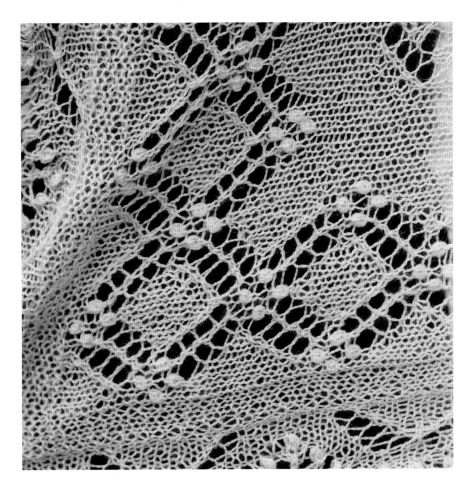

FINISHED MEASUREMENTS

52" square

YARN

Knit Picks Alpaca Cloud (100% Baby Alpaca; 440 yards/50g): Oyster Heather 24807, 5 hanks.

NEEDLES

US 4 (3.5 mm) 47" or longer circular needles, or size to obtain gauge

NOTIONS

Tapestry Needle
Stitch markers

GAUGE

16 sts and 29 rows = 4" in Body lace pattern, blocked

Estonian Square Shawl

Notes:

This Estonian-inspired shawl is knit in one panel with a border that is then picked up and knit in the round.

DIRECTIONS

With smaller needles, CO 193 sts.

Work in Garter st (knit every row) for 10 rows.

On the next row, set up lace: K5, PM, begin working from Body chart on st 1 of row 1, repeating sts 16-27 a total of thirteen times (three repeats are shown on the chart) across the row, then work sts 52-63, PM, K5.

Note that only right side rows are shown: purl across WS (even number) rows.

Work through WS row 30, working the outer 5 uncharted sts in Garter st as established on RS and WS rows.

Rows 31-40: K5, SM, work sts 1-15 from the chart; work in St st (knit on RS rows, P on WS rows) to 15 sts before Garter st marker, work sts 49-63 from the chart, SM, K5. Work Chart rows 31-40 as established.

Rows 41-300: K5, SM, work sts 1-26 of chart row 41, repeat sts 27-36 a total of thirteen times (one repeat is shown), work to end of chart, SM, K5. Working as established, repeat Chart rows 41-60 a total of 13 times.

Rows 301-312: K5, SM, work sts 1-15 from Chart row 61; work in St st to 15 sts before Garter st marker, work sts 49-63 from the chart, SM, K5. Work Chart rows 61-72 as established.

Rows 313-342: K5, SM, work sts 1-15 of Chart row 73, repeat sts 16-27 a total of thirteen times (three repeats are shown), then work sts 52-63, SM, K5. Work Chart rows 73-102 as established.

Work 10 rows in Garter st, removing all markers on final row.

Border

The border is picked up and knit in the round all around the shawl. Beginning with live sts, with RS facing, knit across row evenly decreasing 3 sts, PM (190 sts). Turn clockwise so that adjacent side is facing up. PU and knit 208 sts across the edge of the garter st to the next corner. PM, PU and knit 190 sts across the CO row, PM, and PU and K 208 sts up the remaining garter edge. PM and join to work in the round. 796 sts.

Begin working from Border chart on round 1. Note that only RS rounds (odd numbers) are shown; knit even numbered rounds. *Work sts 1-15, then work sts 16-33 a total of ten times on knitwise ends, and eleven times on row-wise sides, then work sts 34-46, SM. Rep from * for each side to end of round. Work as established through round 19. BO all sts pwise using a needle several sizes larger than gauge needle; this will give a stretchy but even bind off.

Weave in ends, wash and block, pinning out each point in the border.

Legend:

☐ knit
  knit stitch

■ No Stitch
  Placeholder - No stitch made.

⊡ yo
  Yarn Over

◩ ssk
  Slip one stitch as if to knit, Slip another stitch as if to knit. Insert left-hand needle into front of these 2 stitches and knit them together.

◪ k2tog
  Knit two stitches together as one stitch

⊞ nupp
  ((K1, YO) 3 times, K1) into 1 st. Work each K1, YO very loosely to facilitate gathering the sts together. On the following row/round, purl all 7 sts together for the Body, knit all 7 sts together for the Border.

◬ Central Double Dec
  Slip first and second stitches together as if to k2tog. Knit 1 stitch. Pass two slipped stitches over the knit stitch.

Border

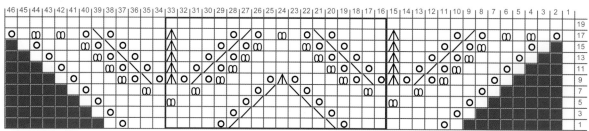

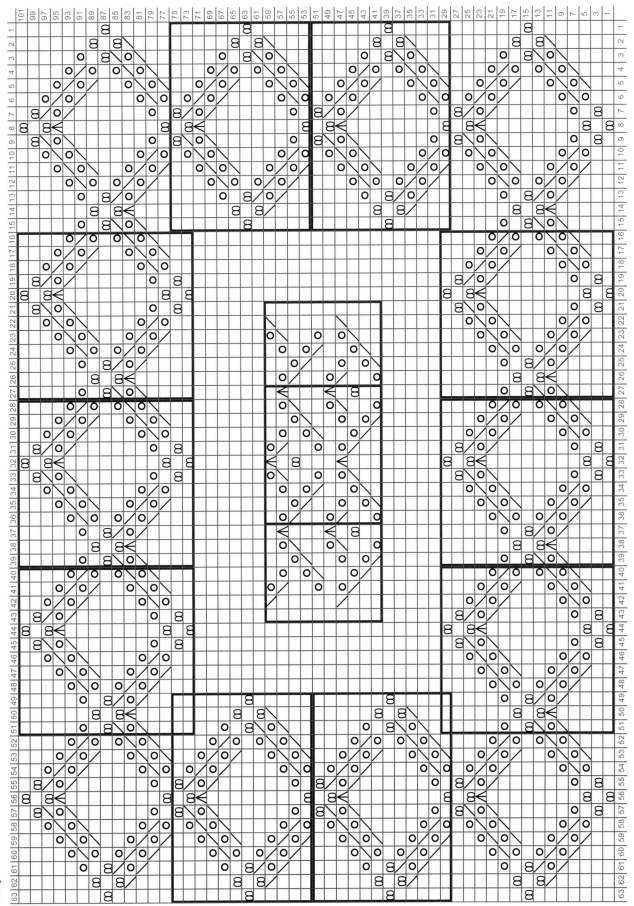

SHETLAND TRIANGLE SHAWL

by Kerin Dimeler-Laurence

FINISHED MEASUREMENTS
32" deep, 74" wingspan

YARN
Knit Picks Palette (100% Peruvian Highland Wool; 231 yards/50g): Sea Grass 26049, 5 balls.

NEEDLES
US 6 (4.0 mm) 32" or longer circular needles, or size to obtain gauge

NOTIONS
Tapestry Needle
Stitch markers

GAUGE
20 sts and 29 rows = 4" in Rings pattern, blocked. Gauge is not critical for this piece

Shetland Triangle Shawl

Notes:

A gusset and shoulder shaping give this shawl its distinctively Shetland shape.

DIRECTIONS

CO 409 sts. Begin working from the Border Chart, working the center 12 st repeat 32 times across. RS (odd number) rows are followed from right to left, and WS (even number) rows from left to right. Work to the last row of the Border Chart; decrease two sts in this row. 407 sts.

Rings Chart Set Up (RS): P1, *(K2tog, YO) twice, K1, P1, K1, (YO, SSK) twice, P1, rep from * 15 times.

Begin working from Rings and Gusset charts

Row 1 (RS): K5, PM, work Rings Chart Set Up over the next 181 sts, PM, work Gusset Chart Row 1 over the next 35 sts, PM, work Rings Chart Set Up over the next 181 sts, PM, K5.

Row 2 (WS): K5, SM, work Rings Chart Row 2 (repeating the 12-st repeat 12 times), work Gusset Chart Row 2, work Rings Chart Row 2 (repeating the 12-st repeat 12 times), SM, K5.

Continue working from both charts, keeping the 5 sts on each edge in Garter st (knit every row), for 144 rows (6 repeats of the 24 rows of the Rings Chart). On each vertical repeat, two fewer repeats of the Rings Chart center 12 sts are worked across the section.

Row 145 (RS): K5, SM, work Shoulder Chart Row 1, work Gusset Chart Row 145, work Shoulder Chart Row 1, SM, K5.

Continue as established through the last row of both charts.

Next Row (WS): K5, P10, P2tog, P to last 5 sts, K5.

Garter Border

The Garter st border along the sides is continued across the remaining live sts of the shawl.

Turn work ready to begin the next row.

Row 1: K4, K2tog, P to 6 sts before end of row, SSK, K4. Turn work.

Row 2: Knit.

Repeat these two rows until 10 sts are left. Break yarn, leaving an 8" tail. Use a yarn needle and the yarn tail to graft the two live sets of 5 sts together.

Finishing

Weave in ends, wash and block, pinning out each point in the border.

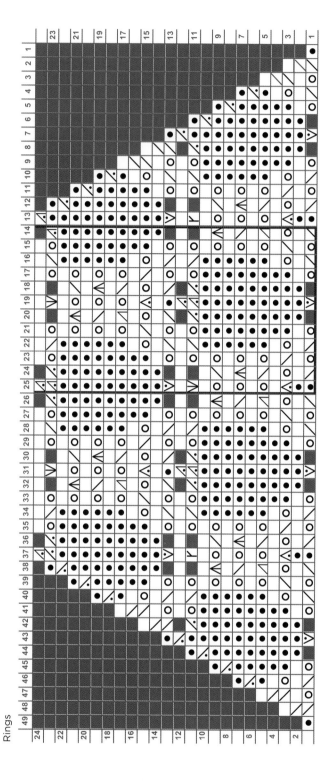

Rings

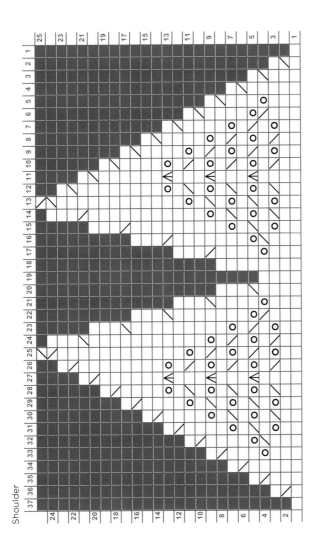

Shoulder

ssk
RS: Slip one stitch as if to knit, Slip another stitch as if to knit. Insert left-hand needle into front of these 2 stitches and knit them together

WS: purl, knit, and purl again all in the same stitch to make 3 sts from 1 & 1st stitches in that order

knit
RS: knit stitch
WS: purl stitch

sl1 p2tog psso
RS: slip 1 stitch, p2tog, then pass slipped stitch over p2tog

WS: slip 1 stitch, k2tog, then pass slipped stitch over k2tog

k3tog
RS: Knit three stitches together as one
WS: Purl three stitches together as one

p2tog
RS: Purl 2 stitches together
WS: Knit 2 stitches together

p2tog tbl
RS: Purl two stitches together in back loops, inserting needle from the left, behind and into the backs of the 2nd & 1st stitches in that order

WS: Slip one stitch as if to knit, Slip another stitch as if to knit. Insert left-hand needle into front of these 2 stitches and knit them together

Central Double Dec
RS: Slip first and second stitches together as if to knit. Knit 1 stitch. Pass two slipped stitches over the knit stitch.

WS: Slip first and second stitches together as it to purl through the back loop. Purl 1 stitch. Pass two slipped stitches over the purl stitch.

Central Double Inc
RS: (k1 through back loop, k1) in one stitch, then insert left needle point behind the vertical strand that runs down between 2 sts just made, and k1 through back loop into this strand to make 3rd stitch of group

WS: (p1 tbl, p1) in 1 st, then p1 into strand between 2 sts just made.

p3tog
RS: Purl three stitches together as one
WS: Knit three stitches together as one

Legend

purl
RS: purl stitch
WS: knit stitch

k2tog
RS: Knit two stitches together as one stitch
WS: Purl 2 stitches together

yo
RS: Yarn Over
WS: Yarn Over

No Stitch
Placeholder - No stitch made.

(k1 p1 k1) in 1 st
RS: knit, purl and knit again all in the same st to make 3 sts from 1 WS: purl, knit, and purl again all in the same stitch to make 3 sts from 1

kfb
RS: knit into the front and back of the next stitch
WS: purl into the front and back of the next stitch

Gusset, part 1

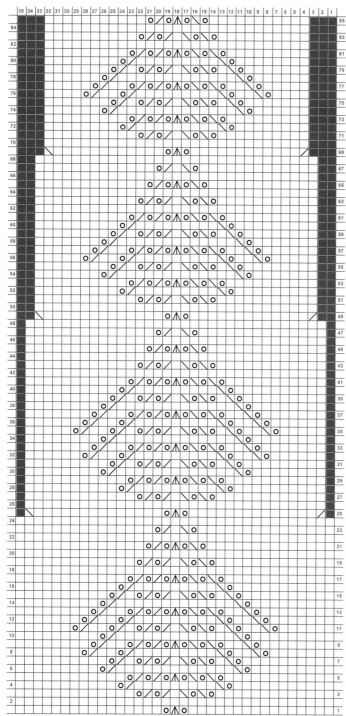

Gusset, part 2

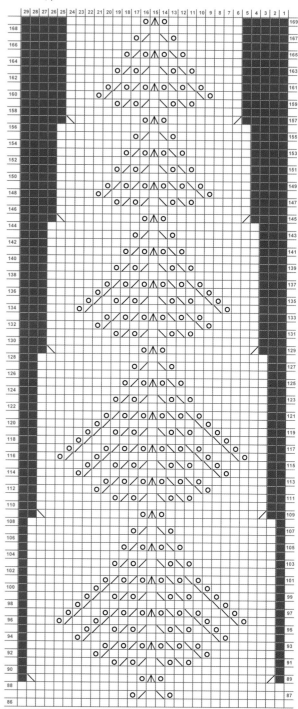

Border

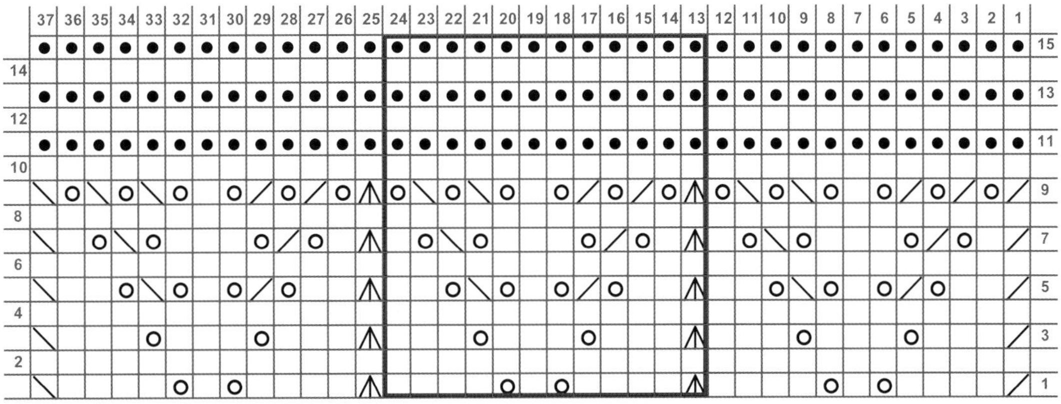
37 36 35 34 33 32 31 30 29 28 27 26 25 24 23 22 21 20 19 18 17 16 15 14 13 12 11 10 9 8 7 6 5 4 3 2 1
15 13 11 9 7 5 3 1
14 12 10 8 6 4 2

PEACOCK SHAWL

by Kerin Dimeler-Laurence

FINISHED MEASUREMENTS
62" diameter

YARN
Knit Picks Gloss Lace (70% Merino Wool, 30% Silk; 440 yards/50g): Bare 24178, 4 balls.

NEEDLES
US 4 (3.5 mm) double-pointed needles plus 24" and 40" circular needles, or size to obtain gauge.

NOTIONS
Tapestry Needle
Stitch markers

GAUGE
15 sts and 22 rows = 4" in Feather, Part 1 lace pattern worked in the round and blocked (gauge is approximate)

Peacock Shawl

Notes:

Waving peacock feathers stem from the center of this circular shawl. The entire shawl after the cast on and set up rounds is charted.

Lace Bind Off

*K2tog TBL, return stitch to LH needle. Repeat from * to end of round. Break yarn and draw through final stitch to fasten off.

DIRECTIONS

Using DPN's, CO 8 sts, PM and join to work in the round being careful not to twist sts. Knit two rounds.

Set-up Rnd 1: KFB in every st. 16 sts.

Set-up Rnd 2: Knit.

Set-up Rnd 3: (K1, YO, K1, PM) 8 times around. 24 sts.

Begin working from the Feather, part 1 chart on round 1, repeating the chart 8 times around. After the last round of part 1, move on to part 2. Repeat chart 8 times around, changing to longer circular needle when sts no longer fit comfortably on current needle.

Note: In rnd 130, you will increase 9 sts into 1 to create the 'eye' of the feather – an 8-st increase. The increased sts are not shown on the chart; work them in St st and work the rest of the chart as shown. Decreases in Rnds 143, 145, and finally 146 eliminate these extra sts.

Border

On the next round, begin working from the Border chart, repeating those 16 sts 46 times around the shawl, placing markers between repeats if desired. After completing round 10, BO all sts loosely using Lace Bind Off.

Finishing

Weave in ends. Wash and block, pinning out all points of the border.

Border

16	15	14	13	12	11	10	9	8	7	6	5	4	3	2	1	
																10
O							Λ							O		9
																8
O	/	O	/	O	/	O	Λ	O	\	O	\	O	\	O		7
																6
O							Λ							O		5
																4
O	/	O	/	O	/	O	Λ	O	\	O	\	O	\	O		3
																2
O							Λ							O		1

Legend

No Stitch
Placeholder - No stitch made.

knit
knit stitch

yo
Yarn Over

k2tog
Knit two stitches together as one stitch

k3tog
Knit three stitches together as one

ssk
Slip one stitch as if to knit, Slip another stitch as if to knit. Insert left-hand needle into front of these 2 stitches and knit them together

Central Double Dec
Slip first and second stitches together as if to knit. Knit 1 stitch. Pass two slipped stitches over the knit stitch.

m9 sts in one
((k1 yo) four times, k1) in one stitch

yo twice
Yarn Over Twice

k3tog tbl
Knit three stitches together through back loops

k5tog
Knit five stitches together as one

Purl
Purl stitch

Feather, part 1

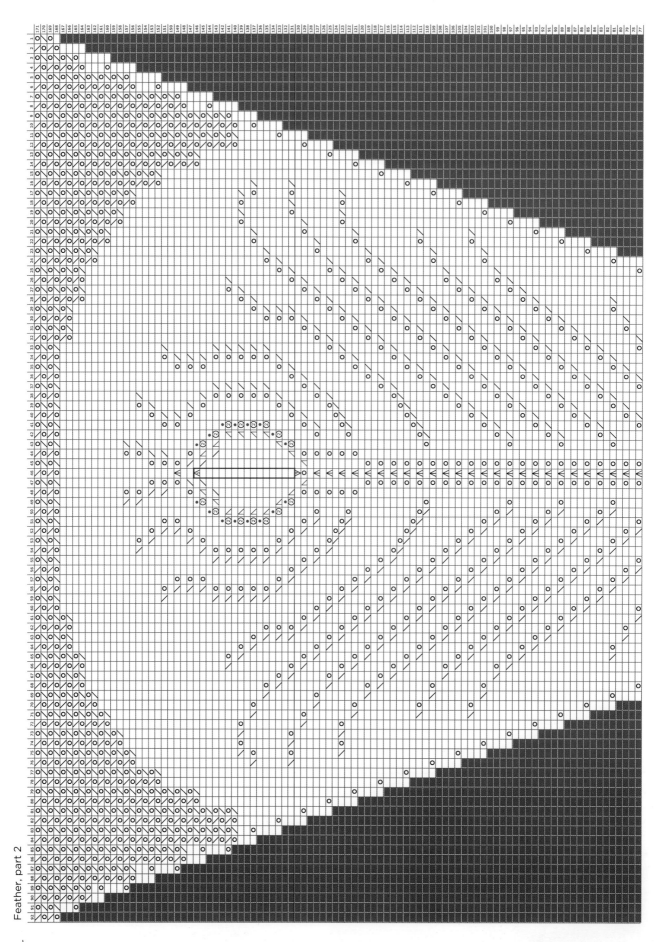

Feather, part 2

VICTORIAN FICHU

by Kerin Dimeler-Laurence

FINISHED MEASUREMENTS
14" deep, 80" wingspan

YARN
Knit Picks Aloft (75% Super Kid Mohair, 25% Silk; 246 yards/25g): Oat 25756, 4 balls.

NEEDLES
US 4 (3.5 mm) 40" or longer circular needles, or size to obtain gauge. You may want to use a 60" circular needle for ruffle cast on.

NOTIONS
Tapestry Needle
Stitch markers

GAUGE
20 sts and 30 rows = 4" in lace pattern, blocked

Victorian Fichu

Notes:

This long, narrow shawl begins with a ruffle. Because a large number of sts are cast on, you may want to use markers to help you count.

W&T (Wrap and Turn):

Work until the stitch to be wrapped. If knitting: bring yarn to the front of the work, slip next st as if to purl, return the yarn to the back; turn work and slip wrapped st onto RH needle. Continue across row. If purling: bring yarn to the back of the work, slip next st as if to purl, return the yarn to the front; turn work and slip wrapped st onto RH needle. Continue across row.

Picking up wraps: Work to the wrapped st. If knitting, insert the RH needle under the wrap(s), then through the wrapped st Kwise. Knit the wrap(s) together with the wrapped st. If purling, slip the wrapped st Pwise onto the RH needle, and use the LH needle to lift the wrap(s) and place them on the RH needle. Slip wrap(s) and unworked st back to LH needle; purl all together through the back loop.

DIRECTIONS

Ruffle

On long circular needles, CO 1600 sts.

Row 1 (RS): Knit.

Row 2 (WS): Purl.

Rows 3-4: Repeat rows 1-2.

Row 5: K2tog across row; 800 sts.

Row 6: Purl.

Row 7: K2tog across row; 400 sts.

Rows 8-11: Knit every row (Garter st).

Body

The body of the shawl is shaped with short rows. Different types of mesh create the patterning. Pick up wrapped sts and work them together with the sts they wrap as you come across them.

Every stitch of the body is charted; there are no repeats. Sections 6 – 10 form one side of the shawl, and Sections 1 – 5 the other. Sections 5 – 6 form the middle. Odd rows are RS rows. Even rows are WS rows.

Begin working from charts on RS Row 1 by knitting across the row to stitch 216 on the Shawl Section 6 chart and then working the W&T . Work back and forth across Shawl Section 5 and Shawl Section 6, incorporating the neighboring charts as rows get longer; first will be Sections 5 and 6, then 4, 5, 6, and 7. Continue as established until finally charts 1-10 are worked sequentially.

Garter Border

After all 90 rows of the body are worked, work 6 rows in Garter st (knit every row). BO all sts loosely.

Finishing

Weave in ends, wash and block, pinning ruffle border into an even ruffle pattern.

Legend

☐ **knit**
RS: knit stitch
WS: purl stitch

■ **No Stitch**
Placeholder - No stitch made.

φ **Wrap & Turn**
RS: Bring yarn to front of work; slip next st pwise. Bring yarn to back; slip st back to LH needle without working, turn work.
WS: With yarn in front of work, slip next st pwise. Bring yarn to back; slip st back to LH needle without working, turn work. Bring yarn to back of work.

• **purl**
RS: purl stitch
WS: knit stitch

○ **yo**
RS: Yarn Over
WS: Yarn Over

╱ **k2tog**
RS: Knit two stitches together as one stitch
WS: Purl 2 stitches together

% **SL 1, YO**
RS: YO, Slip YO from previous row purlwise with yarn in back. 1 stitch inc
WS: Sl YO from previous row purlwise with yarn in front, yarn over. 1 stitch inc

╲ **ssk**
RS: Slip one stitch as if to knit, Slip another stitch as if to knit. Insert left-hand needle into front of these 2 stitches and knit them together
WS: Purl two stitches together in back loops, inserting needle from the left, behind and into the backs of the 2nd & 1st stitches in that order

Shawl Section 9

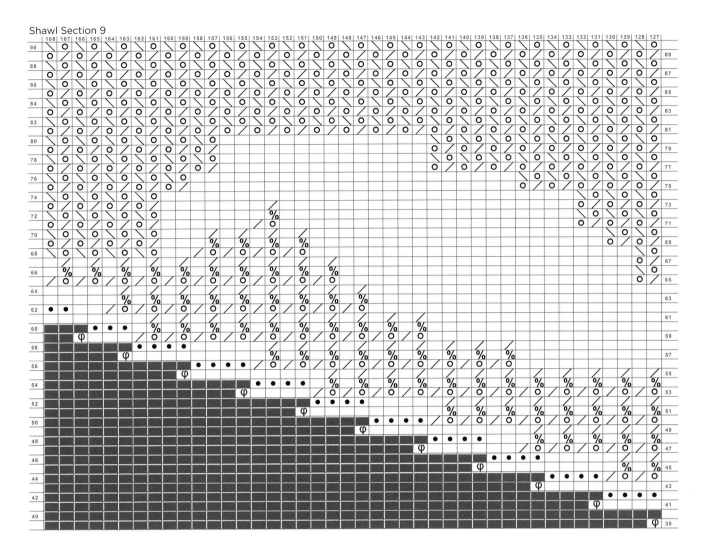

RS rows are read from right to left and WS rows are read from left to right. The chart is split into ten sections that run the width of the shawl They are numbered 1-10, from right to left. Not every row appears in each section.

Shawl Section 10

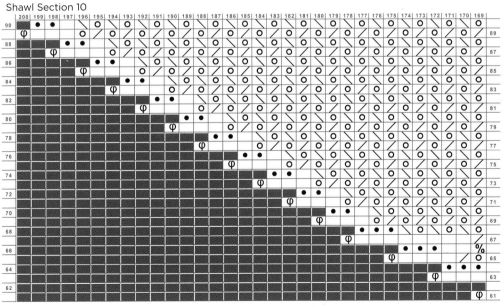

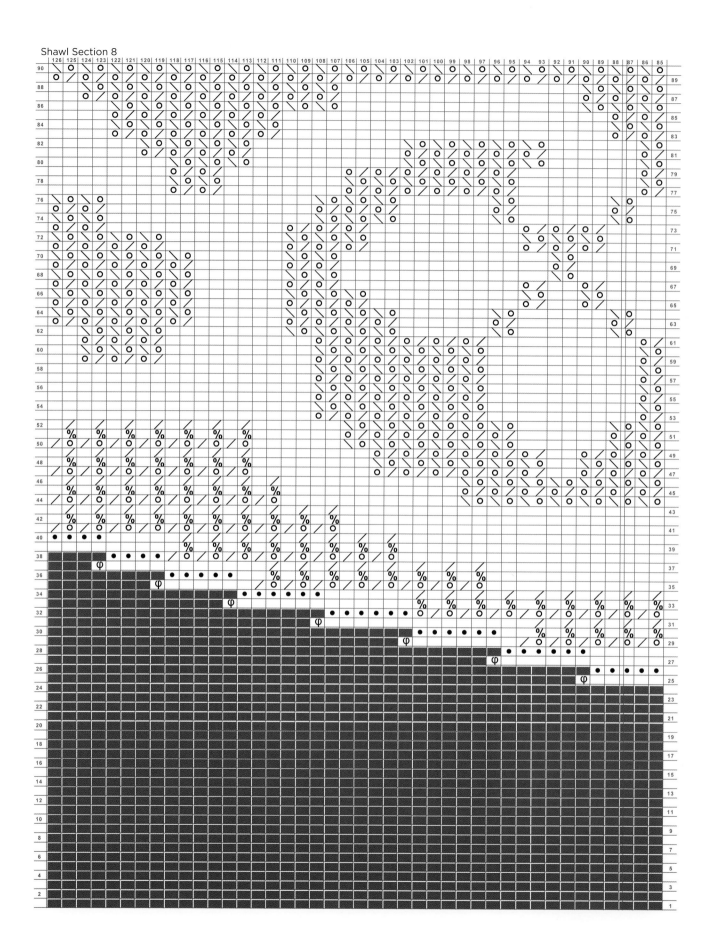

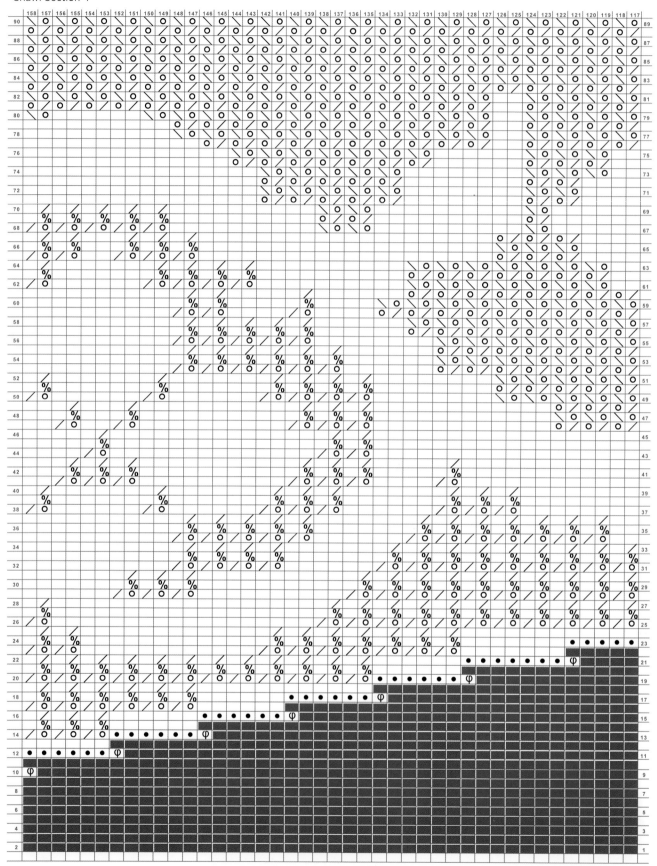

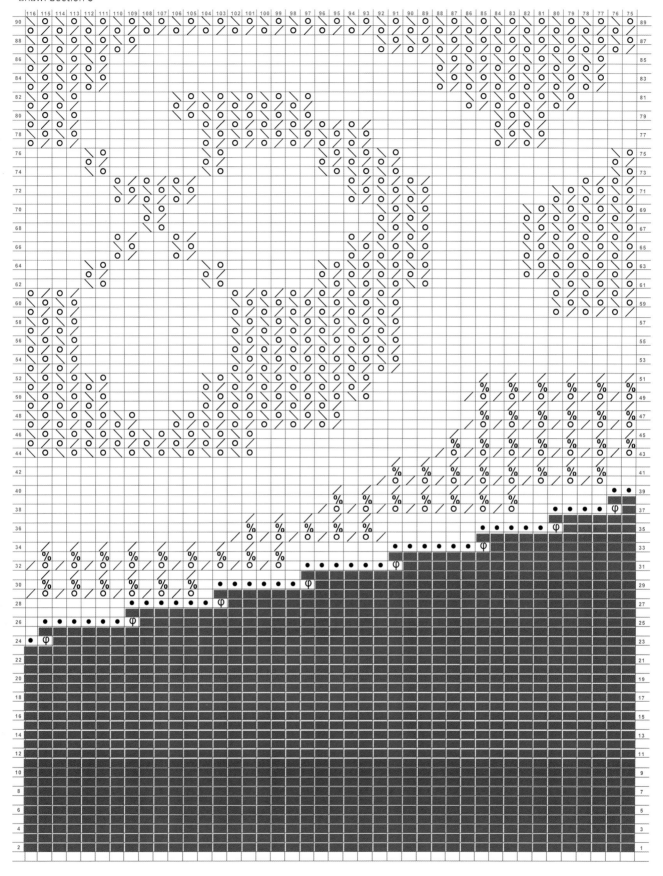

Shawl Section 2

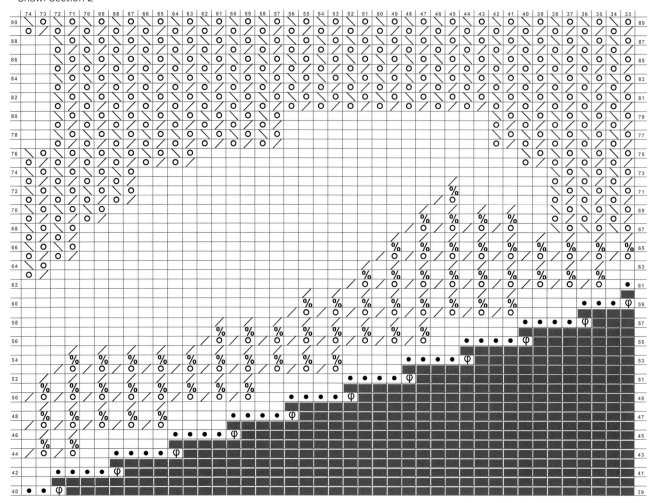

Shawl Section 1

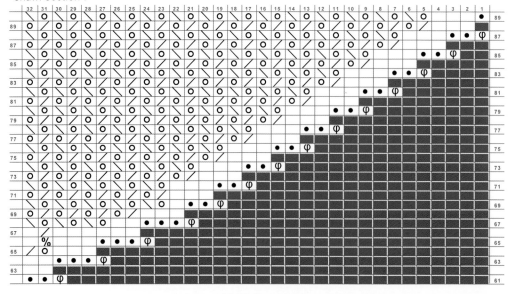

Abbreviations								
BO	bind off	LH	left hand		stitch	TBL	through back loop
cn	cable needle	M	marker	RH	right hand	TFL	through front loop
CC	contrast color	M1	make one stitch	rnd(s)	round(s)	tog	together
CDD	Centered double dec	M1L	make one left-leaning stitch	RS	right side	W&T	wrap & turn (see specific instructions in pattern)
CO	cast on	M1R	make one right-leaning stitch	Sk	skip		
cont	continue			Sk2p	sl 1, k2tog, pass slipped stitch over k2tog: 2 sts dec	WE	work even
dec	decrease(es)	MC	main color			WS	wrong side
DPN(s)	double pointed needle(s)	P	purl	SKP	sl, k, psso: 1 st dec	WYIB	with yarn in back
		P2tog	purl 2 sts together	SL	slip	WYIF	with yarn in front
EOR	every other row	PM	place marker	SM	slip marker	YO	yarn over
inc	increase	PFB	purl into the front and back of stitch	SSK	sl, sl, k these 2 sts tog		
K	knit			SSP	sl, sl, p these 2 sts tog tbl		
K2tog	knit two sts together	PSSO	pass slipped stitch over	SSSK	sl, sl, sl, k these 3 sts tog		
KFB	knit into the front and back of stitch	PU	pick up				
		P-wise	purlwise	St st	stockinette stitch		
K-wise	knitwise	rep	repeat	sts	stitch(es)		
		Rev St st	reverse stockinette				

Knit Picks yarn is both luxe and affordable—a seeming contradiction trounced! But it's not just about the pretty colors; we also care deeply about fiber quality and fair labor practices, leaving you with a gorgeously reliable product you'll turn to time and time again.

THIS COLLECTION FEATURES

Gloss Lace
Lace Weight
70% Merino Wool, 30% Silk

Aloft
Lace Weight
75% Super Kid Mohair, 25% Silk

Alpaca Cloud
Lace Weight
100% Baby Alpaca

Palette
Fingering Weight
100% Peruvian Highland Wool

Shadow
Lace Weight
100% Merino Wool

View these beautiful yarns and
more at www.KnitPicks.com

Knit Picks®

Knitted lace, an intricate craft handed down through the centuries, makes gorgeous garments that stand the test of time. The five patterns in *Heirloom Lace* evoke this rich history. The stoles and shawl patterns bring lace knitting into the modern era with elegant shapes that flatter as they drape. From the whimsy of a Peacock Shawl to the traditional Estonian Square Shawl, every lace knitter will find something beautiful to knit.

$14.99
ISBN 978-1-62767-048-7
51499>

9 781627 670487

32381

PIVOT POINT®

113°
NAILS

ENHANCE YOUR EDUCATION

Augmented Instructions:

Use your mobile device or tablet and any QR-code reader app to scan the target below. This will direct you to the App Store or the Google Play Store to download the Wikitude app, which is used to view our augmented experiences.

When the app is downloaded, find the Wikitude app icon on your device and launch the app.

When opening the Wikitude app for the first time, be sure to allow the app access to the camera on your device.

At the top of the Wikitude app screen, enter "Pivot Point" in the search term window and select "Pivot Point Augmented Experience." The title then appears at the top of your screen.

Now look in the *Pivot Point Fundamentals* books for the icon*. Aim your device so that you see the entire page through your camera. The page will then be augmented so you can view additional content to help you as you work through the lessons.

*Extra augmented content throughout the book is indicated with this icon: